BOOKS OF HOURS

BOOKS OF HOURS

nt astra flebiles ce
li fenestra facti es.
 n regis alta uinu
a et porta lucis ful
gidis micant diem
prennigenti gentes
redempte plaudite.
 aria mater gra
ie mater mie nt nos
ab hoste protege in
hora mortis suscipe.
 loria tibi dinne
qui natus es de uir
gine cum patre et scō

INTRODUCTION

Originally an addition to the end of the Psalter, or Book of Psalms, the first separate Book of Hours known in England was that attributed to the artist William de Brailes, of Oxford, between c. 1230 and 1260. By the end of the thirteenth century the Book of Hours had become the favourite prayerbook of ordinary people throughout Western Europe and in the years that followed its popularity spread and it grew to be a medieval 'bestseller'. Today there are still thousands of Books of Hours scattered throughout the world, providing plenty of scope for collectors, bibliophiles and those interested in illuminated manuscripts. They are probably the most famous of all medieval manuscripts. Often small and highly decorated, these prayerbooks are coveted not only for their decorative value but also for the insight they give into the daily life of the Middle Ages.

The name 'Book of Hours' derives from the practice of reading certain prayers and devotions at the different 'hours' of the day. An 'hour' in the Middle Ages was

PLATE 1
BODLEIAN LIBRARY, MS DOUCE 219-20, FOL. 127

defined as an inexact space of time to be allotted either to religious or to business duties. The monastic orders specified certain prayers and rituals which were to be observed eight times a day and the purpose of a Book of Hours was to enable ordinary people to follow a similar programme of daily devotion. The wide spread of the many books still in existence indicates that they were popular. But the question always arises as to whether they were actually used; the evidence of well-thumbed pages and worn covers suggests that they were. This was not a proper service book, for use in church, but an ordinary person's book of private prayer and meditation, for use alone and at home. We know that some medieval owners read their Books of Hours each morning in bed.

Each Book of Hours is a compendium of different devotional texts. Some are common to every book, some special to particular geographical regions, while others crop up entirely randomly. The core of every manuscript, however, is the section known as the 'Hours of the Virgin', a set series of prayers and psalms, intended to be used in honour of the Virgin Mary at each of the canonical hours of the day ie Matins, Lauds,

PLATE 2
ECOLE NATIONALE SUPÉRIEURE DES BEAUX ARTS, MS 95

Prime, Terce, Sext, None, Vespers and Compline. A calendar listing saints' days and four short readings from the Gospels are also usually present at the front of the book. Two prayers to the Virgin ('*Obsecro te*' and '*O intemerata*') follow the Gospel sequences, preceding the Hours of the Virgin. Then come the Hours of the Cross and the Holy Spirit, which are fairly short and consist of a hymn, an antiphon and a prayer. After this section are the Seven Penitential Psalms with the Litany, and the Office of the Dead, which evolved from the prayers to be said over the coffin. Towards the end of the book one might find the Fifteen Joys of the Virgin, sounding a joyful note after the Office of the Dead and providing an interlude before the important Suffrages, or Invocations of the Saints.

Although many of the elements making up a Book of Hours are standard, the illustrations adorning the pages can vary immensely in quality and richness. By the late Middle Ages the production of illuminated manuscripts was no longer solely the preserve of monastic *scriptoria* but had been taken over by lay scribes and artists who were employed commercially by patrons. The extent

PLATE 3
J PAUL GETTY MUSEUM, MS 7, FOL. 2V

and inventiveness of the decoration must have largely depended on the wealth and taste of the patron who commissioned and paid for the book. Pages are emblazoned with initials in gold and colours and often with miniatures and decorative borders, giving plenty of scope for an imaginative application of colour and pattern. The term 'miniature' originally derives from the Latin *minium*, meaning the red pigment once used by scribes to emphasize initial letters. Its definition was later extended to include pictorial illustrations, not necessarily small in size or displayed in any particular fashion. Initial letters may be either decorative or historiated (containing a small picture within the letter shapes).

The form these illustrative elements took changed over time. The border developed from simple tail-like extensions of initials into sprouting ivy shapes supporting little human figures. Gradually the borders became more and more filled with realistic details until by the end of the fifteenth century they were often entirely formed of naturalistic flowers and animals. In time the miniatures began to contain successive episodes in various stories within a single frame. For instance, incidents such as the Flight into Egypt, which often illustrates Vespers, can be packed with various episodes all of them with a range of different perspectives and viewpoints. Sometimes a book's owners will even be depicted within a miniature, often shown in a devotional position or performing an act of piety. Quality varies from artist to artist while subjects vary from area to area and country to country. Some of the greatest painters of the Middle Ages worked on Books of Hours (including artists as important as Jan Van Eyck and Jean Fouquet) and others we know only by names invented to connect them with some famous work or patron, such as the Boucicaut Master or the Master of John, Duke of Bedford.

Although glamorous and richly decorated Books of Hours certainly exist, many of them obviously commissioned by royal and wealthy patrons (such as the Duc de Berry, the brother of the King of France, who owned at least half a dozen Books of Hours), they were also bought from bookshops by everyday layfolk. Tens of thousands of manuscript Books of Hours must have been made. With the invention of printing an even larger number were produced. In the late Middle Ages piety was an important means of self-expression and ownership of a prayerbook implied status and a sense of respect. Their common currency is demonstrated by the fact that the word 'primer', a first reading book, probably comes from the first Hour of Prime, and the term a 'red letter day' comes from the practice of writing important saints' days in red in a Book of Hours calendar.

In this book the aim has been to show a selection of folios from small Books of Hours, reproducing them at or near their original size and shape. They are grouped in their standard sections and positioned in the order in which they would have appeared. The selection may sometimes seem arbitrary – with so much choice available, it is not always easy to select one page and discard another – but our intention has been to highlight little-known examples and to show the quirky humanity of these manuscripts.

PLATE 4
BODLEIAN LIBRARY, MS DOUCE 219-20, FOL. 128

xv	g	diuisio apostolorū
iiii	a	
	b	Alexij confessoris
xiii	c	
i	d	
	e	Margarete virgis :
ix	f	praxedis virginis
	g	Marie magdalene :
xvii	a	
vi	b	Christine virginis .
	c	Jacobi 7 christofori
xiiii	d	Anne matris marie .
iii	e	
	f	
xi	g	filias 7 simplicis
	a	Abdon 7 sennes :
xix	b	

THE CALENDAR

Always standing at the beginning of a Book of Hours, the calendar lists the saints' days for each month, indicating when celebrations may be appropriate. According to common practice the important Church festivals, such as Christmas and the feast days of the Virgin Mary and the Apostles, are written in gold or red while the lesser festivals and the more minor saints are written in black. The calendar may also give important information about a Book's provenance, highlighting local saints in gold, red or blue and giving prominence to local events such as the consecration of churches and the translation of relics, or even anniversaries of the deaths of notable persons connected with the diocese.

Each month often occupies two pages of a manuscript, and frequently includes illustrations of the labours or occupations of the month, together with their corresponding zodiac signs. The occupations derive from the peasants' seasonal labours and from the pastimes of their feudal lords. For instance, August may be illustrated by a threshing scene and December by killing a pig and preparing food for a long winter.

PLATE 6 JULY

WADDESDON MANOR, MS 26, FOL. 7V

Ianuarius xxxi.
Luna xxx

iii	a	Circũcisio domini
	b	Oct. s. stephani
xi	c	Oct. s. iohannis.
	d	Oct. s. innocentũ
xix	e	
viii	f	Epyphania dni.
	g	ysidon martiris.
xvi	a	
v	b	
	c	
	d	Pauli heremite.
xiii	e	
ii	f	Iuliã & zothia
	f	
x	g	felici presbiteri.

PLATE 8 FEBRUARY
WADDESDON MANOR, MS 26, FOL. 2V

februarius xxviii
Luna xxix

d		Brigide uirginis.
e		purificatio marie
f		Blasii episcopi
g		
a		Agathe uirginis.
b		Amandi theodosii
c		
d		Apollonie uirginis
e		Scolastice uirginis
f		
g		Dominiani confe
b		Juliani martiris
c		Valentini epi m

	d	Longum martyris
	e	
vii	f	Gertrudis virgis.
	g	Theodori episcopi.
xvi	a	Joseph confessoris
iiii	b	
	c	Benedicti abbis.
xii	d	
i	e	Maximi episco.
	f	
ix	g	Annunciatio m
	a	Theodori episco.
xvii	b	Resurrectio dni
vi	c	
	d	Saturnini conf.
xiiii	e	
	f	Pastoris episcopi.

PLATE 10 MARCH

WADDESDON MANOR, MS 26, FOL. 3v

Mayus XXXI
Luna XXX!

vi	b	Philippi Jacobi
	c	
xviii	d	Inuentio crucis
vii	e	Walburgis virg?
	f	
xvi	g	Johannis a p̃l?
v	a	
	b	
viii	c	Trã ẽt. nicolai
ii	d	
	e	Mari ao martyres
x	f	
	g	Seruach episco?
xviii	a	Aquilii episcopi

PLATE 12 MAY
WADDESDON MANOR, MS 26, FOL. 5V

PLATE 13 MAY
VICTORIA AND ALBERT MUSEUM, MS 2538

PLATE 14 JUNE
WADDESDON MANOR, MS 26, FOL. 6V

PLATE 15 JUNE
BRITISH LIBRARY, ADD. MS 18855, FOL. 109

PLATE 16 JULY
BRITISH LIBRARY, ADD. MS 18855, FOL. 109V

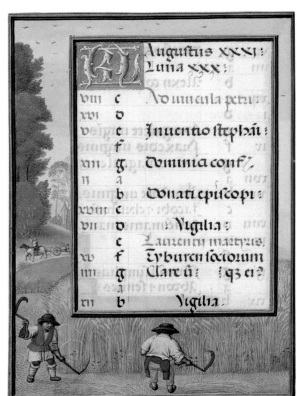

Augustus XXXI
Luna XXX

viii	c	Ad uincula petrii
xvi	d	
v	e	Inuentio stephani
	f	
xiii	g	Dominici conf.
ii	a	
	b	Donati episcopi
xviii	c	
vii	d	Vigilia
	e	Laurentii martyris
xv	f	Tyburcii sociorum
iiii	g	Clare ui̇ pi̇ q̇z ei̇
	a	
xii	b	Vigilia

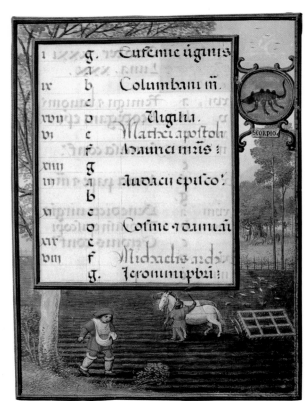

i	g.	Eufemie uginis
x	b	Columbani iii.
	c	
xuii	d	Uigilia.
vi	e	Mathei apostoli
	f	Maurici mris
xiiii	g	
iii	a	Audoeni episco
	b	
xi	c	
	d	Cosme z damiani
xix	e	
viii	f	Michaelis archa
	g.	Jeronimi pbri

SCORPIO

PLATE 20 OCTOBER
VICTORIA AND ALBERT MUSEUM, MS 2538

November xxx.
Luna, xxix.

d		Omnium ſcōrum̄
e		Omnium animarū
f		
g		Euſtaci epiſcopi
a		
b		Leonardi conf̄
c		
d		Quatuor coronator
e		Theodori martiris
f		
g		Martini epiſcopi
a		Liuini c̄ ⁊ mr̄is
b		
c		Clementini mr̄is

PLATE 22 DECEMBER
WADDESDON MANOR, MS 26, FOL. 12

PLATE 23 DECEMBER
BRITISH LIBRARY, ADD. MS 18855, FOL. 108V

Initiu scī euāge
lij. scōm iohēm.
Gloria tibi dūe.
In principio

SEQUENCES FROM THE GOSPELS

The elements which make up a Book of Hours may be divided up into three distinct categories. There are the essential texts, or backbone of the book, which are similar to parts of the Breviary and always appear. They include the Hours of the Virgin and the Office of the Dead. The secondary texts, such as a huge variety of prayers to the Virgin, constitute the flesh, adding colour and variety to the standard texts. And finally the possibility of accessory texts introduces the chance of surprise.

Short readings from the Gospels fit into the second category. They are often present, with short extracts from the narratives of each of the four Evangelists (Matthew, Mark, Luke and John). Each usually begins with a picture of the particular Evangelist writing his Gospel and accompanied by his attribute. (These tend to be an eagle for John, a lion for Mark, an angel for Matthew and an ox for Luke.) They usually appear in their studies, although St John is often shown on his traditional Isle of Patmos.

PLATE 24 ST JOHN
SOTHEBY'S, LONDON

In illo tempore.
Missus est gabriel
angelus a deo in ciuita
tem galilee: cui nomen
nazareth ad virginē despon

PLATE 25 ST LUKE
BRITISH LIBRARY, ADD. MS 20694, FOL. 14

PLATE 26 ST MATTHEW
J PAUL GETTY MUSEUM, MS LUDWIG IX 16, FOL. 35V

In illo tem ſm marcum
pore. Recumbentibus
vndecim diſcipulis apparuit

PRAYERS TO VIRGIN

Especially in Books of Hours made in France, we often find two standard prayers known by their opening words in Latin: *Obsecro te* ('I implore thee') and *O intemerata* ('O matchless one'). These are prayers to the Virgin and help to further the cult of piety towards the Virgin. Both may be introduced by a picture of the Virgin and Child or by a Pietà, although the second prayer is frequently unillustrated. It is common to find a picture of the Book's owner kneeling in prayer at the *Obsecro te*.

PLATE 28
J PAUL GETTY MUSEUM, MS 7, FOL. 2

bſecute do
mina ſanc
ta maria
mater pie
tute plena

PLATE 30
BRITISH LIBRARY, ADD. MS 18852, FOL. 288

PLATE 31
PIERPONT MORGAN LIBRARY, M 729, FOL. 232V

Oratio valde devota

Royne des cieulx glorieuse
mere de dieu & fille precieuse
Je bien a toy mercy quiers
Car tu es la plus heureuse
Et de grace plus plantureuse
Que nul seueur puisse acquerir
Affin que ne puisse perir
De sa mort dentrer perilleuse
Si lennemy me vient ferir
Vieilge bien moy secourir
Au point que dentray mourir
On te auray vaine merveilleuse
Saincte marie prie pour nous
Et pour tous vaincre recheurir
Amen.

nimie
secourir

nimie
secourir

TOUSIOURS EN BIEN ✠ SANS MAL PENCER.

Ad nonam
Deus in ad
iutorium
meum in
tende. Do
mine ad
adiuuandum me festina.
Gloria patri et filio. Spi
rem arator spem mentes
tuorum visita imple
superna gratia que tu creasti
pectora. Memento salutis
auctor quod nostri quondam
corporis ex illibata virgi
na scendo formam sumpse
ris. Maria mater gratie

HOURS OF THE VIRGIN

The most important and indispensable text of all, the Hours of the Virgin constitute the core of a Book of Hours. They consist of a standard series of prayers and psalms intended to be recited in honour of the Virgin Mary at each of the canonical hours of the day.

Each Hour is introduced by a full- or half-page miniature, the subject of which is usually the life of the Virgin. A standard sequence of illustrated scenes might be: Matins – the Annunciation; Lauds – the Visitation; Prime – the Nativity; Tierce – the Angels' Announcement of Christ's Nativity to the Shepherds; Sext – the Adoration of the Magi; None – the Presentation in the Temple; Vespers – the Flight into Egypt and/or the Massacre of the Innocents; Compline – the Coronation of the Virgin. From a devotional point of view, the Annunciation is the most important miniature in the book. Many of the miniatures provide the artist with an opportunity to depict the landscape inhabited by the peasants. Some miniatures can be traced back to well-known, large-scale paintings.

PLATE 33 NONE
BRITISH LIBRARY, ADD. MS 54782, FOL. 126

omme labiaine
aapues.

MATINS

omine labi
a mea apertes
Et os meum
annunciabit laude mea
Eus in adiutou
um meum inten
de. Domine ad adiuuan

eus madiutozium
meuin intende.
omine ad adniuiã
dium me festina. o
oria patri et filio et spũi sčo.

LAUDS

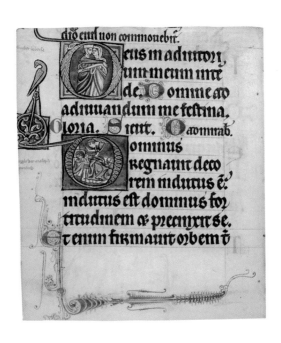

Eus i nomi
ne tuo saluū
me fac: 7 i uir
tute tua libera me. 1
eus exaudi orati
nem meam: auribus
percipe uerba oris 1
mei. m alieni isur
rexerunt aduersum
me: 7 fortes quesiert
anima mea. et non

PRIME

PLATE 39 PRIME

BRITISH LIBRARY, ADD. MS 34294, FOL. 84V

eus Ad primam.
in adiutorium me
um intente. O o
mine adadiuuan

eus in adiutorium
meum intende.
Domine ad ad
iuuandum me festina.

TERCE

eus ad iij
madutonu

eus ad sextam.
maduuorium

SEXT

PLATE 46 SEXT
STOCKHOLM NATIONALMUSEUM, MS 1792, FOL. 35

PLATE 47 SEXT
BRITISH LIBRARY, ADD. MS 17280, FOL. 197V

onine
labia
mea ap[er]
ries. et
os meu[m]
annun
ciabit la[u]
tuam. *Deus in adiuto[ri]u[m]
[m]eu[m] intende. d[omi]ne
ad adiuuandum me festi[na]
Gloria patri. Sicut er[at]
Alleluy a. Inuitatoriu[m]
Aue maria gr[ati]a. plena. do[m]
i[n]us tecu[m]. ps.

NONE

PLATE 49 NONE
BODLEIAN LIBRARY, MS DOUCE 219-20, FOL. 152V

PLATE 50 NONE
ÖSTERREICHISCHE NATIONALBIBLIOTHEK, COD. 1987, FOL. 98V

Ad Uesperas

Eus in adiutorium meum intende : Domine ad adiuuandum me festina. Gloria patri et filio : et spiritu sancto sicut erat in principio et semper

VESPERS

PLATE 52 VESPERS
WASHINGTON LIBRARY OF CONGRESS, FOL. 111V

PLATE 53 VESPERS
NATIONAL GALLERY OF VICTORIA, MS FELTON 1, FOL. 46V

Eus . Jldixprius
in adiutorium me
um intende
Domine ad ad
iuuandum me festina
Gloria pzi et filio z spui sco
ruut erat in pzinapio . etc

COMPLINE

Eusm adiutoriuz
meum intende Dnc
ad adiuuandum
me festina

onuerte nos deus
salutaris noster.
Et auerte iras

HOURS OF THE CROSS AND THE HOLY SPIRIT

Generally appearing after the Hours of the Virgin, the Hours of the Cross and the Holy Spirit are much shorter in length and therefore present less scope for illustration and decoration. Each Hour consists of a hymn, an antiphon and a prayer, but there are no psalms, lessons or responses. These are important themes in Christian devotion and the prayers could be used to supplement the standard hourly prayers. No doubt people read the Hours of the Cross on Good Friday and the Hours of the Holy Ghost at Whitsun, as well as on many other occasions.

PLATE 57
BIBLIOTHÈQUE NATIONALE, MS N.A.LAT. 3055, FOL. 28V

eus inad
uitoruim
mram intende. do
mine ad adiuuan
dum me festma.
lona patri. an

In proprio filio. an
tiphona. Dominus ap
tuit noster p
auxem ego autem
non contradico reuo
sum non abii.

Dorsum meum de
dit percutientibus et
genas meas uellen
tibus faciem. Fac
meum non auerti
ab increpantibus et
conspuentibus in me
Domine deus.

PLATE 60 PRIME
BODLEIAN LIBRARY, MS DOUCE 219-20, FOL. 63V

eus (in)
m adiuto
rium me
um intende Domine
ad adiuuandum
me festina Glo

eus m adm

toiuim me

uui iurende

Omme ab adiuua

dium me festana.

loua pri ꝵ m in

eus in adiu
torium me
um intende
omine ad adiua
dum me festina
loria patri. yn

Eata nobis
passio sit nia
libratio. ut per sam̄
nobis gaudia . prin
ta sint celestia

Loria uro domino
qui pendens in patri
bulo. clamans cum
sit spiritum mundū
et saluans perditum

Dante sonor cristo
pendito et sine causa
predicto. passo mor
tem pro populo. in

erat. aut sum acce
spisset. psalm
super omnes
inimicos meos fact'
sum obprobrium vi
ame meis valde et
amor mortis.
ui vidbant me
foras fugerunt a
me oblinioi datus
sum tanq mortuus
a corde.
actus sum tanq
vas perditum qm

PLATE 64 VESPERS
BODLEIAN LIBRARY, MS DOUCE 219-20, FOL. 85

PLATE 65 COMPLINE
BODLEIAN LIBRARY, MS DOUCE 219-20, FOL. 92

miſerere nos
deus ſalutā
ris noſter z
auerte nam tuam
a nobis.
eus in adiu

PENITENTIAL PSALMS

Constituting one of the basic texts of Books of Hours, the seven Penitential Psalms are a passionate outpouring of grief, consciousness of sin and hope of pardon. King David, traditional author of the Psalms, is said to have committed all Seven Deadly Sins in the course of his long and adventurous life, and to have composed seven special psalms in repentance for each of these sins. The first Penitential Psalm, which opens with the words *Domine, ne in furore tuo arguas me* ('O Lord, rebuke me not in thine anger'), provides an easily recognizable opening to the Psalms.

There are no standard miniatures suitable to illustrate the Penitential Psalms. This means that the variety and scope of illustration used is huge and all sorts of interesting subjects crop up. Since King David was the Psalms' author, an incident from his life is a popular choice. David is often shown as an old man kneeling in penitence with his crown beside him and God or an avenging angel before him. With the changes in iconography in the latter half of the fifteenth century, the theme of David spying on Bathsheba in her bath appears.

PLATE 66
NATIONAL GALLERY OF VICTORIA, MS FELTON 1, FOL. 61

PLATE 67
WALTERS ART GALLERY, MS W 767, FOL. 169V

PLATE 68
FITZWILLIAM MUSEUM, MS 86, FOL. 142

ere dignetis. Et croga
tominibus fideli
bus defunctis requie
eternam donate dig
neris. Et nos exaudire di
gneris. Et croganus
ili dei. E e e croga
gnus dei qui tol
lis peccata mundi.
parce nobis domine
gnus dei qui tol
lis peccata mundi. Et
audi nos domine
gnus dei qui tol

THE LITANY

The Litany of the Saints is one of the essential texts of a Book of Hours and forms an appendix at the end of the Penitential Psalms. The Litany is an extremely ancient form of liturgical prayer and is thought to date back to the earliest days of Christian worship. Its basic purpose is to act as a cry for help, with the text composed of invocations of the Holy Trinity, the Virgin Mary, the Archangels Michael, Gabriel and Raphael, as well as a long stream of saints. Sometimes, as in the calendar, the inclusion of the names of very local saints can help us recognize the district or region for which the book was made. Beginning with the threefold cry for mercy, *Kyrie eleison, Christe eleison, Kyrie eleison*, the Litany has a distinct and separate unity. It is not a highly decorative section and in fact it is unlikely that any miniatures will appear, except for the occasional saint in the margin.

PLATE 70
BODLEIAN LIBRARY, MS DOUCE 219-20, FOL. 210

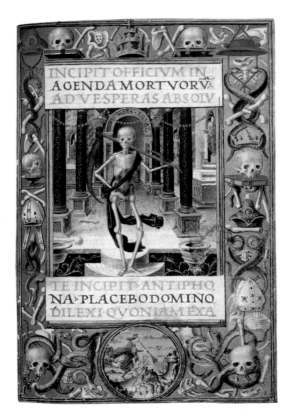

INCIPIT OFFICIVM IN
AGENDA MORTVORV
AD VESPERAS ABSOLV

TE INCIPIT ANTIPHO
NA · PLACEBO DOMINO
DILEXI QVONIAM EXA

OFFICE OF THE DEAD

Celebrated with great pomp and solemnity, funerals were an important part of life in the late Middle Ages.

The service for the Office of the Dead is in two parts: Vespers which are to be spoken in the evening and Matins for the morning. The text consists of prayers originally intended to be said over the coffin as it lies on a bier in a church choir. As far as miniatures are concerned, this is one of the most important sections with a wide and fascinating choice of available subjects. Early manuscripts often have the Last Judgement with angels lifting the souls of the risen dead in a sheet towards Christ. Later on, by the beginning of the fifteenth century, scenes showing the Vigil of the Dead and the saying of prayers over the coffin appear. By the later fifteenth century, the subjects often change to the theme of the imminence and inevitability of death: skeletons prancing with spears, or scenes from the life of Job, the Old Testament patriarch to whom death and destruction were manifestations of the Will of God.

PLATE 71

BRITISH LIBRARY, ADD. MS 50002, FOL. 89

V. Placebo. Ps. VI.

Dilexi quoniam ex-
audiet dominus:
uocem orationis mee.

PLATE 73
BODLEIAN LIBRARY, MS LITURG 41, FOL. 147

PLATE 74
BODLEIAN LIBRARY, MS DOUCE 219-20, FOL. 214

ꝟ. Placebo Psalm
Dilexi quoniam ex
audiet dominus.
uoce oronis mee
Quia inclinauit aurem su
am michi. et in diebʒ meis
inuocabo

PLATE 75

NATIONAL GALLERY OF VICTORIA, MS FELTON 1, FOL. 78V

THE SUFFRAGES

This is often the most profusely illustrated section after
the Hours of the Virgin. It is known either as the
Suffrages or the Memorials of the Saints. It consists of a
series of short devotions comprising antiphon, verse,
response and prayer. In general the series opens with
prayers to the Trinity, which is followed by prayers to
the Virgin Mary, St Michael, St John the Baptist, the
Apostles and then a collection of universal and local
saints. The varying cast of the saints found here
contributes greatly to the individuality and charm of the
books. Each saint appears in the same order as in the
Litany and is identified by a conventional portrait
showing his traditional attributes or emblems.

PLATE 76
BRITISH LIBRARY, ADD. MS 54782, FOL. 55V

Consummatum est. quod sign[...]
ficat labores et dolores quos pro
nobis miseros peccatores su[...]
scepit. teneras iam sumus. tuc
de ingressu anime mee de
corpore meo audiue vocem
illam dulcissimam vocem tua
scilicet vem anima mea dilec
ta mea quia iam disposui tu
as penurias consummari vt
in vt mecum conscendas in re
gno meo epulari iocundari z
commorari per infinita se
culorum secula . Amen . De

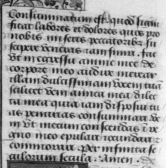

Sancto xpofo. De
sancte xpofo
re martir dei
preciose. Roro
te per nomen
xpi oratoris
tui et per illa
clementiam
quam tibi fecit
quando nomen tuum solus m
rosub te deprecor in noie p̃is

Memoria de tribus regibus

Ab oriente ve-
nerunt ma-
gi in bethle-
em adorare
dominum.
et apertis
thezauris suis preciosa munera obtulerunt aurum si-
cut regi magno thus sicut
deo vero miram sepulture
alleluia alleluia. Reges tharsis
et insule munera offerent.
Reges arrabum et sabba do-
na adducent. Oremus
Deus qui tres magos

Arefacte sunt ia
nue celi vpi mar
tir beato stepha
no qui in numero sanctorum

PLATE 79 ST STEPHEN

KONINKLIJKE BIBLIOTHEEK, MS 74.G.37A, FOL. 9

PLATE 80 ST MARTIN

KONINKLIJKE BIBLIOTHEEK, MS 74.G.37, FOL. 80

SCTA · CATERINA ·

DEVS QVI

Gaudeamus omnes in Domino diem festum celebrantes sub honore beati Nicolai pontificali decoratus infula omnibus se amabilem

PLATE 84 ST MARY MAGDALENE
BRITISH LIBRARY, ADD. MS 34294, FOL. 211V

PLATE 85 ST MARGARET
WALTERS ART GALLERY, MS W 219, FOL. 257

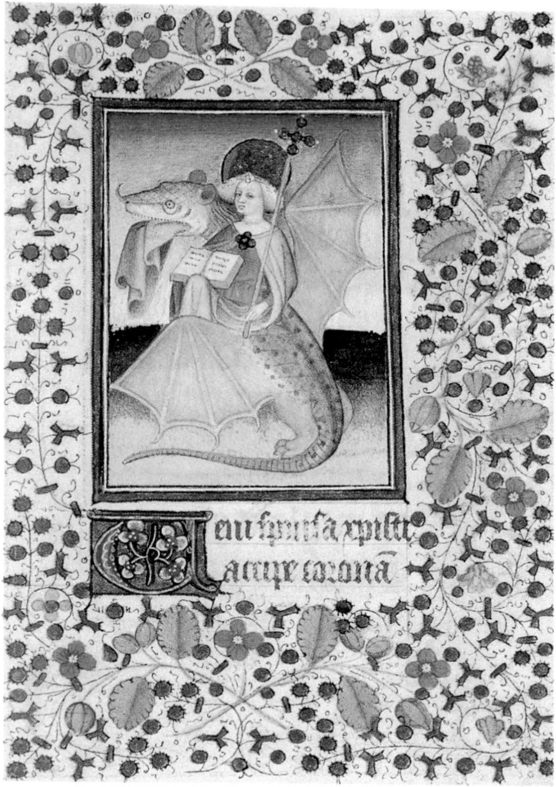
Aue sponsa xpisti
accipe coronā

Manuscripts are listed numerically under source. Plates are listed in folio order thereafter. Unless otherwise stated, images have been supplied by the sources themselves.

BIBLIOTHÈQUE D'ARSENAL, PARIS

MS 291
This Book of Hours was written in Tours in c. 1510-15 and illuminated by the artist known as the Master of Claude de France.
fol. 73v (Plate 69)
The story of David spying on the beautiful Bathsheba as she bathed on a rooftop was a very popular one with Renaissance artists, who often used it to illustrate the Penitential Psalms. After this first sighting David fell in love with Bathsheba, arranged for her husband to be killed in a fearsome battle and married her. She became one of his favourite wives and the mother of Solomon.

BIBLIOTHÈQUE NATIONALE, PARIS

MS n.a.lat. 3055, Hours of Jean sans Peur
The manuscript was made for Jean sans Peur (John the Fearless) who was Duke of Burgundy from 1404 and assasinated in 1419. It was illuminated by the painter now called the Master of Guillebert de Mets.
fol. 28v (Plate 57)
Pentecost commemorates the descent of the Holy Ghost upon the Apostles who have gathered with Mary to receive it (here in the form of a holy dove).

BODLEIAN LIBRARY, OXFORD

MS Douce 219-20, Hours of Engelbert of Nassau
Illuminated in Belgium in about 1485 by the Master of Mary of Burgundy, one of the most admired medieval illuminators. Engelbert of Nassau, whose magnificent monument still stands at Breda, was a Belgian nobleman who served the rulers of the Netherlands faithfully.

fol. 45 (Plate 58)

It is early morning in the Garden of Gethsemane. Christ kneels in prayer while three of the Apostles sleep below.

fol. 56v and 57v (Plate 59)

Surrounded by soldiers bearing torches, Judas steps forward to kiss Christ. The High Priest's servant, Malchus, whose ear had been cut off by St Peter, stands before Christ waiting to be healed.

fol. 63v (Plate 60)

Christ is led before Pilate to hear the charges levelled against him. Pilate is enthroned with a cloth of honour before him and a greyhound at his feet.

fol. 69 (Plate 61)

Christ and Pilate stand together at the top of the steps. Nearly naked, bloodstained after his flagellation and wearing the Crown of Thorns, Christ is being presented to the people who wave their fists and shout 'Crucify him, crucify him'. In the distance, on the right, the procession towards Calvary through the city gates is starting with Christ on horseback flanked by two soldiers.

fol. 74v (Plate 62)

A great crowd has gathered on the hill of Calvary to watch Christ being nailed to the cross.

fol. 79v and 80 (Plate 63)

Christ, his side pierced and bleeding, is on the cross. Below him the Virgin has fainted and is being supported by the Holy Women and St John. The executioners on horseback are shown in the foreground with the city of Jerusalem in the background.

fol. 85 (Plate 64)

A striking border with butterflies and flowers, amongst them orange poppies, scattered on a green ground.

fol. 92 (Plate 65)

In the background is the hill of Calvary with the empty crosses still standing. In the foreground Joseph of Arimathaea and Nicodemus are placing Christ in a tomb in the wall. The Virgin holds his head.

fol. 97v and 98 (Plate 35)

Matins opens with the Annunciation on the left, set in the Virgin

Mary's bedroom, and with a landscape on the right showing the Virgin setting off to visit her cousin, St Elizabeth. The borders are formed of exquisite peacock feathers; the peacock was a symbol of immortality.

fol. 127 (Plate 1)

A page from a sequence of marginal scenes which begins in the Hours of the Cross and runs on into the Hours of the Virgin. Here a fox wearing a cape round its neck sets off for a tournament.

fol. 128 (Plate 4)

A monkey carrying a lance leads the way to the tournament.

fol. 152v (Plate 49)

The Presentation of the Christ Child in the Temple in Jerusalem is shown taking place in a great Gothic cathedral. Simeon the priest is receiving the Child from the Virgin while behind stand a maid and an old man holding candles.

fol. 210 (Plate 70)

A typical medieval marginal drollery, used here in the prayers following the Litany. A crowd of little birds is mobbing an owl, traditionally regarded as the bird of wisdom.

fol. 214 (Plate 74)

The scene shown is the burial of a corpse in a graveyard. The corpse has been wrapped in a shroud and lowered into the ground while a group of mourners in black stands around. A series of niches containing skulls (perhaps representing a charnel house) makes up the border, where the motto of Engelbert of Nassau ('*Ce sera moy*') appears on a scroll.

MS Liturg 41

Probably illustrated by Maître François, the painter of the Wharncliffe Hours (qv), this manuscript originated in Paris.

fol. 147 (Plate 73)

A man lies dying in his bed, attended by his grieving wife and a host of priests and official mourners. The last rites have been administered, just in time since the devil is still trying to drag back the soul as an angel carries it upwards towards heaven.

MS Laud.Misc 188

This manuscript is of English origin and dates from c. 1380-1400.

fol. 143v (Plate 48)

The Presentation of Christ in the Temple.

BRITISH LIBRARY, LONDON

Add. MS 16997

The name of the Boucicaut Master, who illustrated this manuscript, was known for his great masterpiece, a Book of Hours made in c. 1410 for Jean le Meigré, Maréchal de Boucicaut, who was taken prisoner at Agincourt and died in captivity in England in 1421.

fol. 63 (Plate 42)

The shepherds, busy tending their flocks, listen in amazement as the angels tell of the birth of Christ.

fol. 171v (Plate 72)

A colourful portrayal of a grim scene. Priests and mourners chant the Office of the Dead, standing around a coffin draped in a red cloth. This funeral is taking place in a grand medieval chapel.

Add. MS 17280

The artist of this manuscript, who is known as the Master of the Dresden Hours, was one of the most prolific Flemish artists of the last quarter of the fifteenth century. Each part of the Office opens with a double page of decoration.

fol. 197v (Plate 47)

The Adoration of the Magi. The flowers in the border are so true to life that it seems tempting to snatch them from the page. They surround two smaller scenes, the lower one showing the Three Kings on horseback and the one on the left an Old Testament prefiguration of the story. King David is pouring out as an offering to God the water which had been brought to him at heavy cost from within beleaguered Jerusalem.

Add. MS 18852, Joanna the Mad Hours

The owner of this Book of Hours was Joanna of Castile (known as

Joanna the Mad), wife of Philip the Fair, duke of Burgundy. Her
manuscript was illuminated in Bruges in c. 1500.

fol. 288 (Plate 30)
Joanna appears in her own Hours kneeling in prayer opposite a full-
scale miniature of the Virgin and Child. With her is her patron
saint, John the Evangelist. The border on the right includes an early
picture of a clock, then a new and expensive invention.

Add. MS 18855
*Probably illustrated by Simon Bening, the most famous Flemish
manuscript illuminator, this is a collection of pages surviving from
a single manuscript. [Pictures courtesy of Bridgeman Art Library]*

fol. 108 (Plate 9)
In March spring is in the air and people are starting to emerge after
the winter. Noblemen are riding out from the city again with their
hounds, the plough and the garden spade are once more in use and
woodcutters are wielding their axes.

fol. 108v (Plate 23)
The leaves have fallen and a mist hangs over this December scene.
Warmly dressed and ready for action, two huntsmen stand contem-
plating a wild boar which their hounds have just pursued and caught.

fol. 109 (Plate 15)
Everyone is outside enjoying the warm summer air. The courting
couple in the middle of this scene seem oblivious of the activity
around them: the shepherds driving the sheep in to be sheared,
the crowd enjoying a hearty lunch and the travellers setting off on
adventures on horseback and on foot.

fol. 109v (Plate 16)
July is a month of heat and hard work. The peasants toil in the
fields with the scythe and the rake, cutting the hay and loading it
onto farm waggons. A dog lies curled up asleep next to the peasant's
bags. Simon Bening's clever use of perspective is particularly in
evidence here.

Add. MS 20694
Illustrated in central France towards the end of the fifteenth century.

fol. 14 (Plate 25)

The evangelist St Luke is said to have been both a medical doctor and a painter. He is shown here painting a portrait of the Virgin and Child.

Add. MS 34294, Sforza Hours

The Sforza Hours is one of the finest surviving Renaissance manuscripts and has a fascinating history. Most of its lavish illuminations were painted in around 1490 for Bona of Savoy by Giovan Pietro Birago but a large quantity were then stolen. Thirty years later, the Flemish painter Gerard Horenbout executed 16 additional miniatures. The finished Book was probably given as a gift to Emperor Charles V.

fol. 84v (Plate 39)

In the decorated border on the opening page of Prime a putto plays with two rabbits.

fol 199v (Plate 82)

Walking by the sea one day, St Augustine meets a young baby sitting on the shore who is busy scooping water from the sea with a spoon and pouring it into a hole in the sand. When questioned by St Augustine as to the purpose of this exercise, the baby replied that what he was doing was just as futile as trying to explain the Holy Trinity in a book.

fol. 211v (Plate 84)

St Mary Magdalene, after nearly starving to death in the desert, is carried by angels to heaven for nourishment. After years in the desert her clothes have disintegrated but her hair has grown long enough to clothe her. In the background is the pilgrim whose wife she restored to life and whose child she protected after they were abandoned.

fol. 233v (Page 2)

Each of the Penitential Psalms in the Sforza Hours is preceded by a full-page picture of David in penitence. He appears here as a pilgrim, barefoot and clad in a hooded cloak in the middle of the rocky landscape.

Add. MS 38126, Huth Hours
A particularly fine Flemish Book of Hours made in the early 1480s and attributed to Simon Marmion, the panel painter who died in 1489.
fol. 79v (Plate 44)
An unusually large representation of the angel's announcement to the shepherds as they keep watch over their flocks. In the background is a fine medieval bridge; in the foreground is an intelligent-looking dog.

Add. MS 49999, De Brailes Hours
This manuscript is signed by a professional illuminator, 'W. de Brailes', who is very probably William de Brailes, recorded in Oxford in the mid-thirteenth century.
fol. 13v (Plate 37)
In the opening of Lauds the initial displays St Elizabeth embracing the Virgin Mary.

Add. MS 50002, Mirandola Hours
A Book of Hours from Renaissance Italy, the Mirandola Hours was probably made for Galeotto Pico della Mirandola, Prince of Mirandola and his wife Bianca. It dates from c. 1490 and was illustrated by Giovanni Francesco Maineri. It later formed part of John Ruskin's manuscript collection.
fol. 89 (Plate 71)
Death as the Grim Reaper stands in triumph with his scythe within a grand Italian palace. The Latin motto *Omnia mors equat* ('Death makes all equal') appears above his head and the message is underlined by the marginal decoration in which the traditional headgear of the princes of church and state is interspersed with skulls, bones and serpents. At the foot of the page an angel sounds the Last Trump.

Add. MS 54782, Hastings Hours
The Book of Hours of William, Lord Hastings, who was beheaded in 1483.
fol. 43 (Plate 78)

This extraordinary picture provides a colourful border to the Prayers to the Three Kings. It may be that a Christmas tradition of benevolence is being depicted with sacks of gold being emptied onto a crowd who stand below in eager anticipation.

fol. 55v (Plate 76)

St Thomas Becket, the Archbishop of Canterbury, is murdered before the altar in Canterbury Cathedral on 29 December 1170. The cause of his death was his opposition to Henry II's attempts to control the clergy. Surely the most famous event in English medieval history, the inclusion of this miniature here demonstrates the artist's desire to tailor the Book to suit an English buyer.

fol. 85v (Plate 38)

The Virgin Mary, looking tired and weak, is visited by her solicitous cousin Elizabeth.

fol. 126 (Plate 33)

The border shows the royal barge of Edward IV, King of England and patron of Lord Hastings. The motto of the Order of the Garter, '*Honi Soit qui Maly y Pense*', appears on the huge fluttering pennant.

CALOUSTE GULBENKIAN FOUNDATION, LISBON

MS LA 148, Hours of Margaret of Cleves
Made for Margaret of Cleves in c. 1395–1400.

fol. 19v (Page 3)

The Book's owner is shown kneeling before the seated Virgin and Child. Holding a pen in his right hand, the Child is writing the last word of the inscription '*Pater adveniat regnum tuum fiat*'.

ECOLE NATIONALE SUPÉRIEURE DES BEAUX ARTS, PARIS

MS 95

Traditionally attributed to Bourdichon, the miniatures in this Book of Hours are now thought to be by the Master of Claude de France. This suggests that the manuscript dates from the first quarter of the sixteenth century and originates in Tours.

Plate 2

St Geneviève, the patron saint of Paris, appears rarely in Books of Hours. Here she wears a nun's habit and holds a lighted candle that a demon is trying to blow out, symbolizing faith exposed to the attacks of evil.

FITZWILLIAM MUSEUM, CAMBRIDGE

MS 86

An English manuscript dating from c. 1480.

fol. 142 (Plate 68)

King David kneeling in prayer.

J PAUL GETTY MUSEUM, MALIBU

MS Ludwig lx 11, Luxembourg Hours

Dating from c. 1466-70, the Luxembourg Hours originated in northern France or Flanders. The illuminator is known as the Master of Jacques of Luxembourg.

fol. 17v (Plate 27)

St Mark is said to have been sent from Egypt to Rome to write his Gospel there. Here he is working in a medieval scholar's study, with windows opening onto a green and wooded landscape. At his feet is a lion, the emblem of St Mark and later the emblem of the city of Venice which claimed to possess the relics of the saint himself.

fol. 73 (Plate 54)

The Coronation of the Virgin has a richly illuminated border, in which hide a peacock, a moth and a small duck-like creature.

MS Ludwig lx 13

An Italian manuscript from Ferrara which is sometimes known as the Gualenghi d'Este Hours and dates from c. 1470. The illuminators were Taddeo Crivelli and Guglielmo Giraldi.

fol. 3v (Plate 5)

An Annunciation scene used to illustrate Matins in the Hours of the Virgin. Rich with gold and luminous colours, the illumination here has been carried out with imagination and flair.

fol. 187v (Plate 81)
St Katharine stands before a desk reading a prayerbook, with a wheel in her left hand. The wheel, on which she was tortured, represents her martyrdom. (Its presence here serves as a reminder of the derivation of the Katharine Wheel firework.) Only the dog barking below disturbs the sense of calm devotion.

MS Ludwig Ix 16, Strasbourg Hours
An early sixteenth-century Book of Hours from Strasbourg.

fol. 35v (Plate 26)
St Matthew appears in the Bible as a tax collector in Capernaum. Here he is shown in old age, returning to his desk to write the first Gospel. He is attended by the angel who became his iconographic emblem. On the left is a good picture of a medieval cupboard full of manuscripts.

MS 7, Simon de Varie Hours
The owner of this Book of Hours was Simon de Varie, a financial administrator in the district of Bourges. The artist was Jean Fouquet (c. 1420-80), a known panel painter who also worked on manuscripts. The Hours of Simon de Varie have recently been discovered to consist of three separate manuscripts. Two are in the Koninklijke Bibliotheek in The Hague (qv) and the third is this one. The Book dates from a time when Simon de Varie and his family were striving to re-establish themselves in royal favour after a slight falling-out. Hence the choice of Jean Fouquet, the painter to Charles VII himself, to paint certain miniatures for this Book.

fol. 2 (Plate 28)
The Book's owner is shown here kneeling in prayer in a chapel. His coat-of-arms has been partly painted over at a later date. The motto in the upper margin, 'Vie a Mon Desir', is an anagram of his name.

fol. 2v (Plate 3)
An angel and a greyhound support the royal coat of arms. The border, with a realistic trellis from a medieval garden, is of interest since this was the start of the era of domestic gardens.

KONINKLIJKE BIBLIOTHEEK, THE HAGUE

MS 74.G.37a
Both these manuscripts form part of the Hours of Simon de Varie, which is made up of three manuscripts altogether. The third and final manuscript is in the collection of the J Paul Getty Museum (qv).

fol. 9 (Plate 79)
St Stephen was the first martyr. He was stoned to death, it is thought at the instigation of St Paul.

MS 74.G.37
The third part of the Hours of Simon de Varie.

fol. 80 (Plate 80)
One of the most popular saints of the Middle Ages, St Martin was particularly known for this incident in which he met a naked beggar shivering at the gates of Amiens and, dramatically cutting his cloak in two with his sword, handed over one half. Scenes from St Martin's life, including a night-time vision in which he saw Christ wearing his cloak, fill the border.

fol. 84 (Plate 83)
Bishop of Myra in southern Turkey, St Nicholas appears here in his episcopal robes secretly giving dowries to three poor girls. He was known for his beneficence (and is universally regarded as the first Santa Claus) and his powers of thaumaturgy, or miracle-working.

LIBRARY OF CONGRESS, WASHINGTON DC

Edith E Rosenwald Hours
A tiny jewel-like manuscript painted by the Master of the Livre du Sacré de Charles V, a fourteenth-century illuminator who, as his name indicates, worked for King Charles V of France.

fol. 111v (Plate 52)
Joseph leads his family into Egypt. The journey was undertaken in obedience to an angelic message warning Joseph and Mary to take Christ away from Herod's murderous intentions.

METROPOLITAN MUSEUM OF ART, CLOISTERS COLLECTION, NEW YORK

MS 54.1.2., Hours of Jeanne d'Evreux

This manuscript was probably made for Jeanne d'Evreux, Queen of France, in around 1325. It afterwards belonged to King Charles V of France and his brother, the famous Duc de Berry.

fol. 16v (Plate 34)

Matins in the Hours of Jeanne d'Evreux opens with the Annunciation set in an elegant Gothic house, with Gabriel stooping to enter through a low doorway and holding out a scroll inscribed '*Ave Maria*'. The Book's owner is shown kneeling in the initial.

fol. 62 (Plate 43)

The shepherds cower as they are approached by the angel bearing news of the Birth of Christ. The border is filled with peasant figures at work and at play.

fol. 69 (Plate 45)

The Adoration of the Magi appears opposite a full-page miniature of the Crucifixion. Despite the worried expressions on the Kings' faces, the scene is one of rejoicing with angels playing musical instruments in the sky above. In the border below a mother tries to rescue her baby who has been snatched by a scoundrel.

NATIONAL GALLERY OF VICTORIA, MELBOURNE

MS Felton 1, Wharncliffe Hours

French in origin and dating from c. 1475, the Wharncliffe Hours was probably illustrated by Maître François who came from Paris.

fol. 46v (Plate 53)

As Mary and Joseph flee from Bethlehem into Egypt, a pagan statue falls off its pillar, an allusion to a popular apocryphal legend. On the right the Massacre of the Innocents is taking place behind a screen of trees, while the richly illuminated border includes a vivid hunting scene.

fol. 61 (Plate 66)

Nabal's wife Abigail lies in wait for David and his army of men who are approaching with warlike intentions. With the help of a gift of asses laden with food, she was successful in persuading them to turn back. However, before Nabal could learn of his wife's ingenuity, he had died of a heart attack. Soon afterwards David, remembering Abigail's beauty and wisdom, returned to claim her as his wife.

fol. 78v (Plate 75)

Out riding in the forest one day with their dogs and a hawk, three young men encountered three skeletons who claimed that they were themselves. Filled with horror and alarm, the youths fell from their horses and were instantly killed. Two professional mourners in black appear in the border in gloomy attendance. Below, preparations for the burial in a charnel house courtyard are already underway. An emphasis on good deeds bringing salvation is apparent from the act of almsgiving represented on the left.

fol. 114v (Plate 77)

Christopher was a giant of fearsome appearance who spent his life carrying people across a river, lit by a hermit who lived on one bank. Once a child asked to be conveyed across but with each step that Christopher took the child seemed to grow heavier until he was finding it hard to continue. The child then revealed that his passenger had been Christ and that he had carried the weight of the sins of the world upon his shoulders. Christopher became the patron saint of travellers, a particularly important calling since journeys in the Middle Ages were so treacherous.

NATIONALMUSEUM, STOCKHOLM

MS 1792

It is very unusual to find Spanish illuminated work, but this manuscript is a rare example. Dating from c. 1400, it originated near the Catalonian town of Barcelona.

fol. 35 (Plate 46)

The Kings, bearing gifts, have just dismounted at the stable and are preparing to greet the Christ Child. The various small domestic objects, such as the jug and stand, give the stable a homely air.

ÖSTERREICHISCHE NATIONALBIBLIOTHEK, VIENNA

Cod. 1859
An early sixteenth-century manuscript from Antwerp.

fol. 122 (Plate 51)
A pause on the Flight to Egypt. Joseph is gathering water while the Virgin feeds the Christ Child and the donkey enjoys a rest.

Cod. 1987
A Flemish manuscript from Bruges, dating from c. 1460.

fol. 98v (Plate 50)
Christ is being presented in the Temple by his mother and attendants. Yet instead of the lofty pillars of the Temple in Jerusalem, the setting is a late medieval chapel.

PIERPONT MORGAN LIBRARY, NEW YORK

M 454, Hours of Cecilia Gonzaga
This manuscript is Italian and originated in Mantua in the second half of the fifteenth century.

fol. 190 (Plate 40)
The Virgin is attended by two midwives in this Nativity scene. The richly illuminated border contains the arms of Folgiani-Gonzaga.

M 729, Hours of Yolande of Soissons
Owned by Yolande of Soissons, the daughter of a famous crusader, this Book of Hours was illuminated in the late thirteenth century, probably in Amiens, and takes us back to the very earliest period of Books of Hours.

fol. 232v (Plate 31)
The Book's owner appears in the setting of a Gothic chapel, kneeling before a statue of the Virgin and Child which seems to be coming to life before her. Yolande's dog has entered the chapel with her and is sitting at her feet.

SIR JOHN SOANE'S MUSEUM, LONDON

MS 4, Soane Hours

Although the exact provenance of this manuscript is not known, it is thought to be German in origin and to date from the sixteenth century.

fol. 98 (Plate 55)

Here, in exquisite detail, the Coronation of the Virgin Mary in heaven is depicted. The Holy Dove hovers above and the angels stand behind in willing attendance.

SOTHEBY'S, LONDON

A manuscript from Rouen, dating from c. 1465.

Plate 24

St John is sitting on the Greek island of Patmos writing his Gospel. However, the devil is creeping up behind, hoping to steal his inkpot and stop his literary efforts.

VICTORIA AND ALBERT MUSEUM, LONDON

MS 2538

Painted by Simon Bening (1483-1561), one of the most famous of all manuscript painters, this incomplete manuscript is sometimes known as the Salting Hours. All the pages shown here are detached leaves.

Plate 11

The warm April weather has enticed courting couples and families out into the flower-filled meadows. Strolling or playing the mandolin, they are enjoying their leisure while behind the peasants are busy herding the sheep, milking the cows and ploughing the fields.

Plate 13

In the Middle Ages, the first day of May was an occasion for joyful festivities. A boat decorated with branches of may and filled with nobles celebrating is about to pass below a bridge on which a group of horses and their riders are returning from the forest. Seemingly oblivious to all the scenes of excitement, a woman carries on with her laundry from the steps.

Plate 19

A busy bucolic September scene in which two figures are making a start on a field of corn while two others, their sickles at their sides, take a refreshment break.

Plate 20

A picture of bustling activity in which the fields are being ploughed, seed sown, swine herded and acorns knocked down from the trees for them to eat. Only a lonely figure stands idle at the gate to the field, watching it all happen.

WADDESDON MANOR, AYLESBURY

MS 26

Dating from c. 1540, this manuscript comes from a Bruges workshop.

fol. 1v (Plate 7)

The roof of the house is still covered in snow but a hearty fire is blazing in the hearth and the master, still clad in his fur-trimmed coat, is warming himself before it. Behind him a maid lays the table for supper.

fol. 2v (Plate 8)

Warmly dressed to combat the cold February winds, two peasants are pruning the vines and setting up trellises in preparation for the spring. Behind them the field slopes down to a lake around which nestle a few fairytale castles.

fol. 3v (Plate 10)

A small patch of blue sky has appeared and there are a few leaves on the trees at the start of March. Even the nobles have ventured outside to stroll in their neat and well-trimmed garden and, from the other side of the fence, to observe the gardeners toiling over the digging. In conventional style, the appropriate zodiac sign is shown at the top of the page.

fol. 5v (Plate 12)

Their boat decked in fresh boughs of may and covered in a scarlet canopy, two rather solemn-looking ladies are being rowed along the river in celebration of the May morning. As they float they sing to the accompaniment of a pipe.

fol. 6v (Plate 14)

In June everyone is willing to linger out of doors, enjoying the warm breezes, the flowers and the spectacle of the sheep-shearing. This sheep looks particularly docile.

fol. 7v (Plate 6)

The docile cart horses wait patiently while the farm waggon is loaded with hay in this July scene.

fol. 8 (Plate 17)

In the heat of the day two peasants are about to take their scythes to a golden field of corn, which is bordered by poppies and a few bright blue cornflowers. Their harvest is bundled into sheaves and taken away on a waggon.

fol. 9 (Plate 18)

A flock of birds follows the plough as it digs deep furrows through the muddy field. Autumn is in the air as one farmer scatters his seed, while another shakes down acorns from the trees for the pigs.

fol. 11v (Plate 21)

The cycle of the seasons has come round again. The trees are bare, the sky is grey and the peasants have come in from the fields to beat the flax and winnow the corn.

fol. 12 (Plate 22)

The snow lies thick upon the ground and is still falling fast but this does not deter the peasants from their seasonal task of killing the boar in preparation for a Christmas feast.

WALTERS ART GALLERY, BALTIMORE

MS W 90

An early fourteenth-century Book of Hours, originating in Northern France.

fol. 61v (Plate 41)

A Nativity scene in which the Virgin rests on her bed, tended by a tired Joseph, as the ox and ass guard the Christ Child.

MS W 96

This elegant manuscript, with its formal background and delicate border, is characteristic of late fourteenth-century Parisian work.

fol. 50 (Plate 36)

Lauds opens with a miniature of the Visitation. When the Virgin Mary arrived at her cousin's house, St Elizabeth fell to her knees and greeted her and at that moment the Christ Child leaped in his mother's womb (Luke 1:41). Mary then spoke the famous canticle, the Magnificat, 'My soul doth magnify the Lord'.

MS W 219

A manuscript from eastern France, dating from the 1420s.

fol. 257 (Plate 85)

In the late Middle Ages Margaret belonged to a group of extremely popular saints. The patron saint of childbirth, her story was a colourful one. Her punishment for rejecting the attentions of the Roman prefect Olybius was torture and a spell in prison where the devil, in the form of a dragon, swallowed her. The cross she carried, however, upset the beast's stomach which then mysteriously opened and ejected her to safety.

MS W 220

This Book of Hours was illuminated in Bruges in about 1450.

fol. 138 (Plate 29)

The owner, a young man wearing his best robe, is portrayed kneeling before the Virgin and Child in a fashionable domestic interior with the family silver laid out on display on the sideboard. The text begins with the prayer to the Virgin, '*Obsecro te domina sancta*' ('I beseech you, holy lady').

MS W 222

Owned by the Poitiers family and made in Amiens in c. 1465.

fol. 1v (Plate 32)

The entire Tourotte family appears here in prayer, with Pierre Tourotte and their son in front and Antoinette Tourotte behind with their daughter, attended by their patron saints. The initial 'T' is incorporated into the border.

MS W 223

Dating from c. 1465 and originating in France, probably in Poitiers.

fol. 76 (Plate 56)

The Coronation of the Virgin is the most frequent illustration for
Compline. It appears again here as a miniature, with further
illustrations in the borders showing the death of the Virgin and her
Assumption, another theme that is sometimes used for Compline.

MS W 767

*Made for the Adimari family of Florence, this manuscript dates from the
early 1460s.*

fol. 169v (Plate 67)

The life of David, and the depiction of his various sins, dominates
the miniatures used for the Penitential Psalms. Here the artist,
Zanobi Strozzi, has chosen to illustrate David's slaughter of Goliath,
a picture of youthful triumph which often appears. A young blond
David stands upon the Philistine's giant body; in his right hand he
holds a sling and bloody sword and in his left Goliath's head,
dripping blood.

Phaidon Press Limited
Regent's Wharf
All Saints Street
London N1 9PA

First published 1996
© 1996 Phaidon Press Limited

ISBN 0 7148 3464 5

A CIP catalogue record for this book is available from the
British Library.

Printed in Hong Kong

Page 2 BRITISH LIBRARY, ADD. MS 34294, FOL. 233V

Page 3 CALOUSTE GULBENKIAN FOUNDATION, MS LA 148, FOL. 19V